Beautiful

Donna Dissauer Saliba

Table of Contents

Dedication

This book is lovingly dedicated to my goddaughter, Rayna Grace Schultz.

Introduction

The poems in my second volume of poetry all have wonderful meaning to me. I have chosen poems that have very clear messages and important thoughts. I have chosen a red rose to feature on the cover, as one of the meanings behind a red rose is strength. I will carry the same theme throughout the book.

One poem is written for my goddaughter, Rayna Grace Schultz. It was an honor to be chosen.

I believe that the poems in this volume speak words of strength and wisdom, something I want not only Rayna, but every other person, to be blessed with. Along with strength and wisdom, my hope is that the poetry in this volume also teaches them to enjoy the beauty of life. For no particular reason, the last several poems are about water. I know that water relaxes me, whether it is listening to a river run, or the waves coming up hitting rocks. To me water is therapeutic; therefore its therapy is to lend strength. I thought I would share that with you.

I loved writing the poems in this book and hope you all enjoy reading them.

Acknowledgments

As always, I truly appreciate all the help of my father, Gerald Dissauer. I could never have done this, or any other book, without him. I have never seen a man with more patience in all the times I changed things. I'm looking forward to our next project!

I have several photo credits to include in Beautiful You. They include, in no particular order, Gerald Dissauer, Ellen Davidson, Ian Eichinger, Lissa Eichinger, Joel Eichinger, www.photobucket.com and www.freefoto.com. What pictures I could, I supplied myself. I had very specific ideas of what I wanted for each picture and poem and the photos supplied certainly delivered. Thank you and love to all of you!

A special acknowledgment goes to both my cousin Mark Eichinger and his niece, Lissa Eichinger for their blessing to share the poem "Ike" in this book. Both of your families are very special to me and the memories are priceless! God bless you both.

I also want to acknowledge my husband, Robert Saliba, for his support and appreciation for my poetry and everything else I do and stand for. I'll love you always!

Beautiful You

I look into your eyes
Beyond a million tears
To see you begging
To rid you of your fears

I look at your mouth
Beyond a tired frown
To see you wondering
When you'll wear your crown

I look into your heart
Beyond its breaking beats
To see you asking
If you can endure the heat

I look at your hands
Beyond their aching joints
To see them praying
Your anguished mind to anoint

I look into your soul
Beyond its hopeful feeling
To see you anticipating
Its eventual healing

I look into
All these parts of you
And see nothing less
Than beautiful you

My Goddaughter

Welcome to my life
Little Rayna Grace
What a pleasure it is
To see your eyes and angel face

May you always find yourself
Standing proud and strong
May the praises sent your way
Become a beautiful song

May all the shooting stars
Light your future roads
May all your dreams
Be lovingly bestowed

May all the wishes made
Come true one and all
May your faith so strong
Catch you if you fall

May I always be there
Every time you need
May we pray together
A prayer God is sure to heed

Dedicated to my goddaughter, Rayna Grace Schultz, born May 24, 2004

Ike

He was our husband, father, brother, cousin.
But,
Different than
The man we once knew.
He left strong and able,
Came home tired and worn
His spirit different than before.
Lord,
I pray,
Bring him home.
Give him
The measure of peace
He deserved.
Let your tired child
Rest in your loving embrace
So he feels your love
Breathes the life-giving breath of you
And let comfort
Be his forever more.

This poem is in loving memory of my cousin, John Paul Eichinger, who everyone called "Ike".
May God bless you and keep you, cousin... United States Army, Vietnam Veteran

Don't Ask Why

Don't ask why
When you see tears in my eyes.
Hold me,
Promise to never leave.
Your strength
Is all I need.
Hope
Is the gift you give to me,
And life is what I feel
With you near.
The chance
To really feel alive
Carries me through my day,
As the wind
Guides a tattered, crumbly leaf
Over a mid October evening.
Floating
On your love alone.

With You Forever

I see the tears
In your eyes,
Feel the pain in your heart.
I hear you
Begging for a fresh start,
Pleading for forgiveness.
Ask no more.
My love is yours
To keep in your heart
For all of time,
Just as my hope is.
I pray for you
Day in and day out,
To make the right choices.
That you choose to see the sun,
Rather than
A passing dark cloud.

Humble Beginnings

His clothes tattered and torn,
His belly empty and aching,
The look on his face forlorn,
He spent the evenings pacing.

The soles of shoes used to catch
On the shack's bare wooden floor.
He was always keeping watch,
Always hoping for more.

Flies buzzed in and out
Through the broken window.
And after the awful measles bout,
There were three less siblings in tow.

The vile stench of poverty
Wallowed in the air,
The fading thought of liberty
It just didn't seem fair...

Now grandpa sits upon his front porch swing
Eyes glistening with humble tears,
He's worked hard and gained many things,
In his eighty one years.

Transformation

A rose in bloom
To cheer up a room,
Sunshine after a storm
To keep the earth warm.

Refrain from seeing death
As life's last breath.
It is merely a change,
Of being someplace strange.

Keep your head up, not down
Wear a smile, rather than a frown.
Look up toward sunny blue skies,
Dry your tear-filled eyes.

For the one you love
Is watching you from above
From a place with a view
So grand and new.

It is merely a transformation
Another kind of creation,
To help the one that you adore,
Keep you forever more.

His Spirit Lives On

He sat at the window
Wondering why
The whitetail deer
Never mulled about his yard.
Still,
Everyday he sat,
Waiting
For the beautiful creatures to show.
One rainy afternoon,
God called his child home.
Final respects were paid,
Still the whitetail deer
Didn't mull about his yard.
As his family gathered around,
Speaking idle chat,
Old memories surfaced
About the elusive deer.
As they turned to peer out the window
Toward the backyard,
There they were.
An entire family of whitetail deer
Mulling about his yard.
Comforted at the sight of them
They thought amongst themselves,
His spirit lives on.
And they smiled that day.

In The Present

Wrapped in the present
Of a new day.
Wrapped in the present
Of earthbound rain.
Wrapped in the present
Of a child's smiling face.
Wrapped in the present
Of a lover's beguiling gaze.
Wrapped in the present
Of a joyful tear.
Wrapped in the present
Of a bountiful year.
Tied in a bow
These gifts come to me.
Fastened with a ribbon,
Kept close to my heart.
Showered with confetti,
Each day
Is a gift from those
Who love me in return.
Mother Earth,
Mother Nature,
Child mine,
My love,
My heart.

Reasons

If the reasons I care
Could be laid in a line,
They would wrap the earth
Over a thousand times.

If the reasons could be written
In the finest of books,
Millions would read it
To take a close look.

If the reasons were a harmony
Sung to a crowd,
It would take hours to sing
And be applauded so loud.

If the reasons were stars
Shining high in the sky,
They would send a brilliant
Warm light to your eyes.

If the reasons were raindrops
Falling to the ground,
They would refresh
With strength newly found.

The reasons I care
Are all nestled in my heart,
To be remembered so dearly
If we're ever apart.

Keep the reasons close to your soul
My love,
Your life will be peaceful
As a soaring white dove.

My Hopes For This Year

My hopes
For the birth of this new year
Are just a few.
Some simple,
Others harder to come by.
Each scene changing easily;
Bright colors waltzing in life's kaleidoscope.
Reaching for the stars,
Grasping to every bit of hope.
Waiting for love to be born,
And the conception of big plans.
To sip champagne from a crystal flute,
And feel the tingling sensation
From tongue to stomach.
To feel ocean spray
Upon my face
And to taste the salt

Upon my sunburned lips.
To gallop on horseback
Along the ocean's shore,
Beating my rival
By the length of a stallion's neck.
A newborn baby
Resting a sleepy head
Upon my shoulder.
To jump in a pile
Of dry, crumbly leaves,
Like the first time
I ever did as a child.
Watching snowflakes
Whirl about a winter landscape
And putting another log
Upon a crackling fire.

The Song Of My Life

My love for him
Is the song of my life.
A powerful choir
Singing love's praise.
High and low voices
Chanting a chorus of love.
To all who hear,
The powerful songs
Raise the hope of singing
About their love
To a higher power.
The song of my life
Is the pride and joy
That I feel for my love,
And the way
I help him to grow.
He is the song of my life
And I sing
With a fervent voice
To the heavens.

The Heart Of Music

Guitar strings that seem to sing
A tune, a timeless tale
The sound plays into my ears
The harmony is resonating

The plink of piano keys
Keep happily playing
As butterflies
Waltz with the breeze

The beating drum
Pounding out the rhythm
Pulsation felt from under the floor
My pumping heart feels every thump

The strumming beauty of the harp
Soft and light and wonderful
Graceful yet strong
The hum of harmony fills my heart

The beating of my heart is a symphony
Playing the music of my life
Every instrument a chorus
Each tune an epiphany

Make every day a masterpiece
An orchestral time of pleasure
A harmonious day of music
To fill your life with peace

On Mended Wings

Learning to fly
Again on your own
A life once disrupted
How much you have grown

As an eagle
Soars through the skies
Gone are the tears
That fell when you cried

On mended wings
You soar from this place
Showing how able you are
So full of grace

Gone are the days
You wished would just end
Your heart
Has long been on the mend

This day you woke up
And as a bolt from the blue
You fly on mended wings
To heights you never knew

You now have your freedom
To fly as you desire
Up over the clouds
Higher and higher

Musical Kaleidoscope

Blurred and hazy,
Like the chalk that has been lifted
From the sidewalk
By chilly autumn rain.
Puddles
Become melting pots.
Colors bleed into one another,
As a kaleidoscope
Turning and dancing
To the tune of a melody.
Colors intermingle
And hide behind each other,
Becoming one in the same
Then separate again.
As notes in a chord
Joining together,
To make music.
One note stands alone again
To bring a different sound.
Each turn of the kaleidoscope
Is a new way
To look at things,
Such as life and colors
And music.
Beautiful when alone,
Orchestral when combined.

As A Pressed Rose

Take advantage not
Of relationships in life.
Be there for each other
During troubled times.
You never know
How long or short
The gift of life will last.
Relationships are fragile,
Like the most delicate china.
So precious it is,
It should be handled
With the utmost care
And gentleness.
Like the wings
Of a fluttering monarch,
Torn apart
Would be the means of survival

If broken.
As relationships would
If not given the tender love
Or understanding they need.
Preserve a friend or loved one.
To press
A fragrant rose
Between the pages of a book.
Let caring and gentleness
Be the pages
The rose is enveloped in,
And touch it with the same
Kindness and gentleness
As you would
Delicate china
Or the wings
Of a carefree monarch.

A Tribute To Mom and Dad

Mom and Dad,

A tribute to you
To say thanks
For your never-ending love
And the kind things you do.

Since the day I was born
You've watched me grow
From your little girl into a woman;
Our family ties will never be torn.

Now as I start a new chapter,
The love you have given me,
I will share with my husband
So we can live happily ever after.

The road to this day has been long,
Our destination has been reached.
Join my new husband and me
As we sing our wedding song.

So on my wedding day,
I wanted you to know
Just how much I love you both
In each and every way.

Love,

Your little girl

Showers of Light:

(Watching the meteor showers in the early morning hours.)

Our senses are keen
As we walk through the park
In the darkness
Bathed in a starlit gleam.

Chill blankets the night;
Cool and crisp
Is the cloudless sky.
Everything is just right.

Look up to the sky
To see the brilliant
Showers of light,
High above the earth they fly.

We're covered with plastic ponchos,
Gathering around
In the middle of the park,
For one incredible show.

Stars shooting this way and that;
White strobes against the black
Leaving a trail of white smoke,
But its awesome effect smothers fast…

THANKSGIVING 2005

Pride In Freedom

It started as a distant dream
In our forefathers minds
New laws of freedom written
Liberation was now color blind.

Freedom for all who came
To unsettled frontier land
They were to be citizens
United they would stand.

Red white yellow and black
The colors of their skin
Standing together as one
There was nothing they couldn't win.

Red white and blue
The colors of Old Glory
The stars and stripes them selves
Hold many untold stories.

Two hundred some years later
Still waving proud and tall
Is the same grand testament
That no one can make us fall.

My Comfort

You are my smile
When I am too weak.
After a while with you,
Joy returns to me.
You become my grabber,
When I
Can no longer reach or bend.
My driver,
When I can no longer see the road.
You are my longing hope,
When my health starts to go awry.
You are my support,
When I feel I cannot go on.
You are a younger version of my self;
My image forty years ago
Or maybe more…
You become a living memorial to me,
Liking what I like,
Doing as I do.
You return my will to go on
With the gentle touch of your hand,
Or the smile on your face.
The meal that you prepare.
My own you love as your own.
As I grow tired,
You are my energy;
Increasing
My desire to enjoy
Another moment with you,
Another smile,
One more cup of coffee…

Ode To The Aged

A fleeting thought…

A lesson taught

Without the memory

It seems for naught...

Various Shades of Brown

We all have the power to heal
And certainly the ability to feel
It is not about a race
Or the color of one's face
But it is what's in the heart
The need for all to do their part
It's about the need to work together
Make our corner of the world better
It is about one's ability to inspire
Success that comes from one's inner fire
It's not about who can draw a crowd
But it's about making each other proud
It is teaching our children right from wrong
That will make our future sure and strong
It is about calming someone else's fears
Walking hand in hand throughout the years
We are all a common people
Strong and able not weak or feeble
It matters not whether we wear a crown
When we're all various shades of brown

Everyday Is A Holiday

She wore her smile
As proudly
As fine jewelry
For all to admire.
The smile that she wore everyday;
Graced all with
The beauty that lived within her.
It spilled out of her,
As a million rays of sun
Illuminated the earth.
Fingers of warmth gently comfort you.
She lit up our lives,
Tenderly warmed our hearts.
The holidays
Are embodied with her spirit
So that
Every moment spent with her
Was
A holiday to remember forever,
Or a memory to hold to
And be comforted by.
Everyday will be a holiday,
A chance to embrace her spirit
And keep her forever.

In loving memory of Judith Epstein.

Masterpiece

The sun is soaked up
By the sky
The entire expanse
Drips into the horizon
Drains into the lake
Through the honey, blazing colored autumn trees
To saturate the ground
A melting pot of colors
Dripping through the landscape
That graces my vision
And fills my heart with hope
A watercolor painting
One color mixes with the next
Signed with love
By the artist that painted
A masterpiece

A Day in The Life Of Me

My heart beats in time
To thoughts going through my head
Jammed with a million things
I have to do each day
So many to care for
In what seems a moment's time
A hug to greet with
A kiss to say goodbye
See you tomorrow
Said a hundred times a day
Going here and there
Floor by floor I make my way
Caring for one and all
Every hour of the day
Just a simple gesture
To let each know I care
As I leave to go home each day
My thoughts are still with them
I wave my hand to all I meet
And bid them a good night

Winter Solstice

Winter's first day
Brings with it a thin sheet of ice
Blanketing the earth in a frosty chill
The sun does little
To warm frozen fingers and toes
As it wraps the earth
With its icy grip
Breathing frozen breath in your face
Winter winds
Whirl back and forth around with
Unrelenting force
A rose
Frozen in place
Its red petals standing defiantly against
Winter's stone cold fury

Kati

Antique doll
With locks of gold
And cheeks of rose
Tell to me your tale untold…

Haiku

(Five Seven Five syllable verses)

Freezing winter day
Light of sun is dwindling
Long season ahead

White and puffy clouds
Fill the blue and endless skies
On summer mornings

Butterflies tickle
Land softly on a petal
Wings full of splendor

Neon blue skies fill
Autumn dusk as dark covers
The light with curtains

Whitetail deer grazing
Pawing gently in the lea
Wildflowers dancing

Leaves dancing about
Falling from their master trees
Coloring the ground

Bunnies bounce outdoors
Enjoying crisp autumn air
Birds in flight go by

Winter storm blowing
Little flakes of pure white snow
Melting on my gloves

Salty water drops
Land upon my sunburned face
On the briny shore

Little sparrows come
To chirp a song of new life
When spring is just born

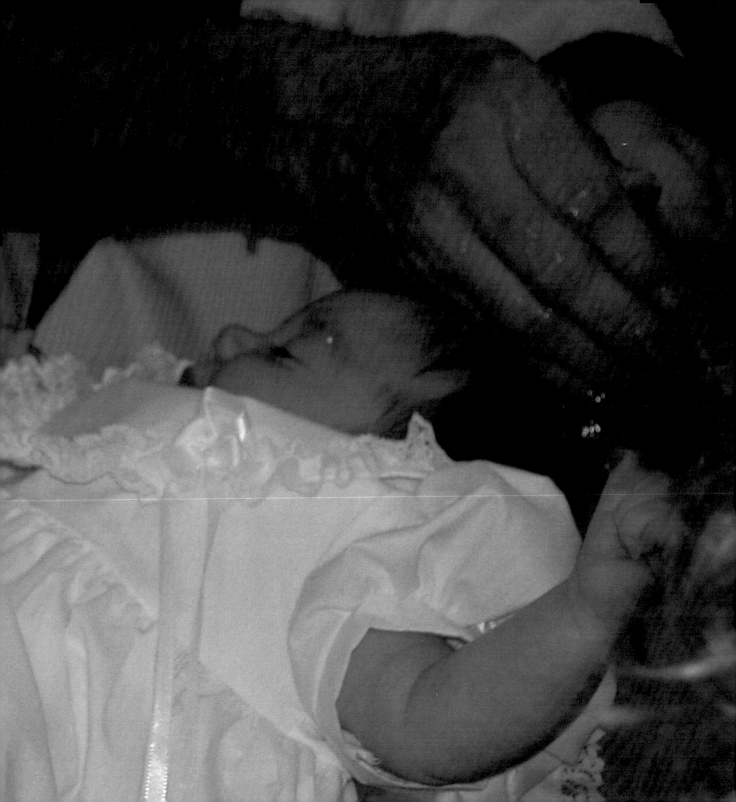

Wanting

A desire so distinct
Tangible
It squeezes the heart and soul
Rendering it breathless
Unmercifully making one wait longer
To get
What is wanted
Baby
Tiny hands reaching for tenderness
Long awaited happiness
Chirping birds on a spring morning
Finally
New life
Presents itself to you
Basking
In the radiant glow of sunshine
All is fresh and new
Full of life
Just as baby birds are in spring
Is a baby
Peacefully resting in your arms

No Losers

It has been said
Life's a race against time
One step
Ahead of everyone else
Pounding feet running a race
Is the beating
Of
My heart
In a race against myself
Ten steps ahead
Of where I really am
In a race with no finish line
No opponents or proponents
Just myself
As I race toward my goals
I know what I want
What it will take
To finish
A race I can't lose

In the Park

Washed in the rain
Dried in the sun
Time spent at the park
For some catch and a run

Toss the ball
And I'll chase the ring
We'll have all the fun
A day in the park can bring

Let's greet all the pups
The elder dogs too
Just sit and relax
I have a toy to chew

We can romp and play together
What joy we will show
All our canine friends
We're so happy to know

Let's have a lap of water
It's okay if we splash
When we get back home
We'll be asleep in a flash

What a day at the dog park
We're all wagging our tails
A couple hours of fun
To bring joy it never fails

Blessings

Blessings blow around the earth
On winds dancing across the lea
As the sun shines down
To light the day
Wind will send blessings your way
The stars shine on high at midnight
To drowsy earth below
Blessings illuminate the earth
As a mom tenderly loves a child
So do blessings love a heart
As ballerinas leap across the stage
So do blessings
Finding their way to your life
Making their way
As if through a crowd
To bless you with strength
As many drops of water fill
Each and every ocean
Or rays of sun drench the earth
And light your eyes
Dandelion feathers flutter through the air
Each carry sweet blessings
Your way

Grandma and Grandpa

A loving pat
A tray of sweets
A set of chipped china
To enjoy a savory feast

A classy silver tea service
To ponder yesterday
Holding special memories
As they slowly make their way

An older pair of glasses
Sits perched upon their noses
An old set of furniture
Adorned with golden roses

A chest full of memories
To remember all the years
A pair of crystal flutes
They used to celebrate the cheers

Grandma and Grandpa
They are the most special of all
Their job is to inspire you
And encourage you to stand tall

Atlantic Sunrise

Waking up
To the warm tender kiss
Of the rising sun
Hugged by the light of dawn
Slowly rising from slumber
Senses rise
With the light of day
Sun cuts through the night
Scythes slicing black satin
Slowly embracing
The blue Atlantic waters
As the foamy white waves
Slowly arise
Beginning their journey toward shore
Life awakens
In the light
Of an Atlantic sunrise
Rocks and shells
Lay upon the bed of wet sand
Slumber until
A collector embraces them
I awoke this morning
To the kiss
Of the rising sun

Droopy

Loving and soulful
Relaxed and sleepy
Sunday mornings
A favorite time
Louis Armstrong on the radio
His easy tunes
Emulate the mood
Naps aplenty
On the sunny spot in front
Of the window
The same look on his face
For whatever he wants
A foot warmer
After a long day at work
Loving you
More than loving himself
The essence of your best friend
The epitome of loyalty
And trust
The right idea of a good life
Naps, play, a good meal
And plenty of love
To go around

Soul Searching

In the farthest depths
Of feelings
Lies the epitome of happiness
As grand as a far reaching horizon
Delicate line under the blazing sun
The search for true happiness
Lies within the soul
Warming like the fire of the sun
Inviting
As a gracious hostess
All encompassing
Tender protector with arms of steel
And a heart of gold
Knowing truth and happiness is found
In the farthest depths of the soul

Can I Keep You

So long my tender angel,
Be light of heart
And fancy free;
As a fluttering butterfly
Dancing on
The luscious scent of roses;
Waltzing on the heavenly fragranced breeze
That now smells like your beauty.
You place kisses,
Barely felt on my cheek;
Feather-like wings
Give a gentle wind
That mimics the way
You touched my heart.
The essence of your spirit
Embodies the kindness of your actions;
You are the gentle wind
And warming sun.
The dew on a spring flower
That captures your spirit,
And forever keeps you with me.
Godspeed my tender angel.

Rainy Sunset

Neon pink against dismal grey,
An odd contrast.
Drizzle falling from the sky
Merge with tears
Falling from my eyes.
Like a drop from the faucet.
Building
Slowly, slowly.
Walking the roads
With nobody's hand to hold.
Waiting to meet someone,
Raindrops falling to greet the earth;
Clouds lying on a green hilltop.
The luxurious bed of grass
Smells even sweeter
By tears from weeping clouds.
Something odd
With sunsets such as these,
Dim
And full of color.
The promise
Of a love to meet,
Tomorrow to greet,
To smell the scents so sweet.
The vows of tomorrow's promises,
Spoken this evening.

Keep the Rose Alive

My heart is filled
With your love,
My soul cries out for more.
The perfect marriage
Of quality and quantity.
The beauty
Of love lies
In the quality of the emotion.
Filled no more
With empty gestures and false promises.
Eyes wet
With tears of happiness
Thriving on the love of you,
My heart and soul
Are filled to capacity.
Yet,
You always give me more.
Your love
Spills out of me
Lake the fragrance from a rose.
The love of you lingers,
And the sun that shines
Is the glow of my happiness,
Enabling me
To nurture you in return.
The sunlight
Is yours as well,
And the scent of love hovering near
Will last forever more.
But still,
I cry out for more.
You are the sun
Keeping my rose in bloom.

AMERICAN

EDUCATOR

This book is
the property
of
_____
_____
_____

ducation commences at the mother's knee,
d every word spoken within the hear-
g of little children tends towards the
rmation of character.   —Ballou

owledge is of two kinds. We know
subject ourselves, or we know where
we can find information upon it.
—Samuel Johnson

Building Bridges

Ignorance
Is the dam
It acts as a deteriorating bridge.
The bridge
Between bigotry and harmony,
Hate and love.
It becomes impassable,
For ignorance holds back education,
Segregating
The different ones.
Education
Shows how to cross the broken bridge.
It makes the bridge strong.
Once cannot
Cross from hate to love,
When ignorance
Acts as a dam
That blocks the flowing waters
Of knowledge.
Education builds the bridge,
Lets negative become positive
So enemies turn into allies.
Opposing sides can finally unite
Into the strongest of armies,
Graduate
To harmony;
Like scholars who teach students
How to build bridges.

Veranda

On the east coast
For a vacation in July,
On the veranda of the beach house,
Amid salty air,
A promise I made to me.
To myself I would always be true,
And find one
Who was true as well.
My best friend
To grow old with;
Our hearts would beat
Forever as one,
Together,
As colors meld together
Into interesting hues.
Complimenting,
Falling in love;
Falling together.

Beautiful Garden

Garden of red roses
Fragrantly tickling noses
Waltzing with the winds
A droplet of dew glistens
Garden of pink carnations
Sweet smelling sensations
Dancing with the dandelions
Proving an alliance
Garden of yellow tulips
The senses do flips
Prancing with the peonies
With the utmost ease
A true Garden of Eden
All senses will be risen
Mother Nature's children
The joy they give you golden
Through the garden taking a walk
One can almost hear them talk
Through the swishing of the trees
Putting your soul at ease

Tribute

Thoughts of you
Linger in my mind.
The scent of you
Drifts through my senses.
Your kindness
Surrounds my being.
A tribute
To the one I love,
Who will forever be with me.
An image of you
Is what I can see,
Every time
Into a mirror I stare.
Our love
Combined you with me,
I with you.
So close were we
That I feel you in my presence,
You became my aura.
I smell you
In the fragrance of the rosebush,
Hear you
In he pitter patter of the rain.
See you in the sun drenched sky,
Taste your love
In the sweetest nourishment.
A tribute
To the one who became me,
The one who I became,
Whose love is present
Forever in my senses.

Age of Gold

Drifting on the memory
Of yesterday,
Holding tight to your love's hand
As time here nears its end.
On a magical swing of emotion,
And the romance of yesterday.
Age of gold is precious,
Age of gold is you.
Loved so completely,
Set to be invaluable,
Priceless.
Touching a life
With golden sunshine,
The warmth of your kindness
Emulating afterlife.
Whole once again,
And forever more.
Wings tipped with gold
The sense of your love
Washes over us with angelic radiance.
Blessed
By the age of gold,
Blessed by you.

Reunion

Two of the same family,
Yet different shades.
Different hats.
A reunion of the blues;
Of sky at water
Being brought together.
It is merely an image.
For they have never met.
If only it was
The way that it seems.
Where do the waters end
And the skies begin?
At the reunion on the horizon.
It seems the water
Is colored
By the hue of the sky;
As a child's life his
By his parents.
Water changes with the sky,
Pink with the setting sun,
Blue as it shines on high.
Water is grey with sadness
On days of overcast.
Smiling and shimmering
When sun comes out to play.
A reunion on the horizon
With the laugh of a dolphin
And the chirp of a bird.
Until the sun
Kisses the water goodnight.

Ocean View

Ocean spray,
Tingly upon my face;
Frosty dew on warm earth.
Water
Reflecting sky and sun,
Rippled by waves
Lapping at the shore.
Quenching the thirsty sand.
White birds dot the azure sky.
Slowly moving,
Snowy white clouds;
As gently moving sailboats across the water.
A natural mirror
To project a perfect image.
The ocean always changes.
What is silent and calm one moment,
Turns to a raging beast the next;
Peaceful water awakens
And becomes
Something that churns wildly.
Attacking,
Until silently the beast sleeps.

Embracing

Bright day
With skies of azure.
Seashells strewn across
The ivory sand,
Kissed by the blue sea
As it rushes to embrace.
A joyous reunion
Of sand and water.
On the sunny strip,
Heard are the chirps
Of birds in flight,
Searching for a destination.
There seems to be none.
The water stretches far
Beyond the point of sight.
Only seen
Is the horizon.
As sky hugs the water
With protecting arms.
The wind;
Master of the sky
That sends the water;
The water that quenches the thirsty sand.
The sand upon which lays
The shells to nap.
Upon which descending birds land,
Still searching for a destination.

Acre Lake

A crystal clear looking glass
Ensconced with wild grass
The pond is motionless
Timeless
Time is standing still
No breezes through the windmill
Life under water can flourish
The plants beneath will nourish
In their water filled galaxy
The lack of life a fallacy
With the blue heron's wish
For lunch to catch a fish
And the croaking bullfrogs
Prey on creatures near the bog
Water reflects the sun rays
Shimmering diamonds on a silver tray
A backyard pond
With nature has a bond
The looking glass so clear
Many forms of life are near

Niagara Falls

Hear the river running.
For the secrecy lying within
Is ever so cunning;
Her water never runs thin.

For just up ahead
Of this silent river,
Are falls that are fed
With silence that withers.

Pounding, roaring waters
Surrounding the mist.
Blessed were our forefathers
To receive such a gift.

Blue water turns to white
As it rolls over the edge.
Putting up a fight,
Giving a heaven sent message.

That one
Cannot control
The one
That cannot be controlled.

Our Niagara Falls.
Not one person
Can ignore its thunderous calls
For any reason.

Look with wonder
At its awesome power
During the summer
From a nearby tower.

During the winter
Listen to the muted sound,
As the quiet river
Gradually begins to resound.

When Niagara calls
The river
Over its great falls,
The heart begins to quiver.

Old Faithful

The geyser
Bursts forth,
Old Faithful
Rising up to kiss the sky.
Like the meeting of lover's lips,
Every kiss is like the first.
Powerful.
Like a gallant knight
Rising up to the fight,
Water rises higher and higher.
Louder and more forceful,
Until quietly it slumbers.

Royal

The expanse of the lake,
Royal in hue,
Wears
A cloak and crown
Of icy jewels.
Sun drenched snow
Bounces light
In every direction;
During
The frigid grasp
Of winter's desire.
A picture of royal beauty,
A colorful prism
Fashioned from cut crystal
Of ice and snow,
Water and sun.

Get Published, Inc!
Thorofare, NJ 08086
25 February, 2010
BA2010056